The Let's Talk Library™

Let's Talk About
Poison Ivy

Melanie Apel Gordon

The Rosen Publishing Group's

PowerKids Press™
New York

To Lisa and Rob, Jen and Michael, Judi and Glenn. With love, Melanie

Published in 2000 by The Rosen Publishing Group, Inc.
29 East 21st Street, New York, NY 10010

First Edition

Book Design: Erin McKenna

Photo Credits and Photo Illustrations: pp. 4, 8, 12, 15 by Suzanne Mapes; p. 7 © Custom Medical Stock; pp. 11, 20 by Carrie Ann Grippo; p. 16 © J. S. Reid and Wedoworth/Custom Medical Stock; p. 19 © J. S. Reid/Custom Medical Stock.

Gordon, Melanie Apel.
    Let's talk about poison ivy / by Melanie Apel Gordon.
        p.   cm.—(The let's talk library)
    Includes index.
    Summary: Discusses how to identify poison ivy, how to prevent getting a rash, what the rash looks and feels like, and how best to let it heal.
    ISBN 0-8239-5415-3
    1. Poison ivy—Juvenile literature.   [1. Poison ivy. 2. First aid.] I. Title. II. Series.
RA1250.G67 1998
616.5—dc21   98-41328
                                                                                  CIP
                                                                                  AC

Manufactured in the United States of America

12.25

Contents

Camping

Livvy and John are on a camping trip with their family. All week they have been fishing, hiking, and swimming. At night they sleep in tents. Livvy and John like to explore nature. Today Livvy found a beautiful plant. "Look what I found," she said to John, pointing to a bunch of dark, shiny leaves. John reached down to pick some of the pretty leaves. "Don't touch that!" his mom said. "That's **poison ivy**! If you touch it, it will give you an itchy rash."

◄ *Spending time outside is lots of fun. Just be careful of the surprises nature may have for you!*

Pretty Leaves, Flowers, and Berries

When you're in the woods or playing in a field, there might be poison ivy around. Keep your eye out and look for these **characteristics**. Poison ivy grows close to the ground. Its leaves are tear-shaped and grow in groups of three. Poison ivy's leaves are shiny and change colors throughout the year. In spring they are yellow-green, in summer they are dark green, and in fall they become reddish. In summer and early fall, greenish white berries grow on the underside of poison ivy leaves.

This poison ivy plant has already begun to change colors. See how shiny the leaves are? ▶

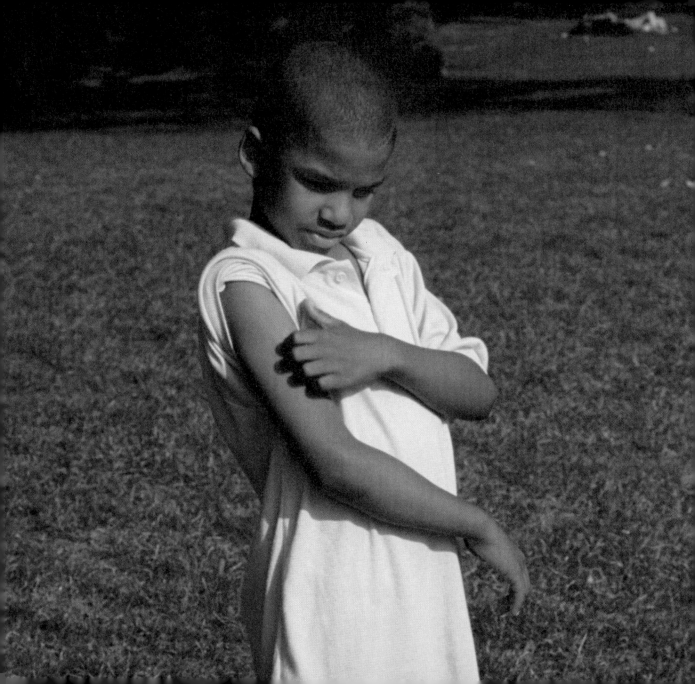

Itch! Itch!

In poison ivy leaves, roots, and stems is an oil called **urushiol**. Most people get an itchy rash if they touch this oil. If you get the rash, try not to scratch it. Just scratching the rash won't spread it, but there may still be urushiol on your skin when you have the rash. If you scratch and get some urushiol on your hands, you can spread it to other parts of your body, or even to other people. And it's not nice to share your rash.

 Scratching your skin too much can cause dirt or germs to get into your rash.

The Rash

You get a rash from urushiol because your body is **allergic** to it. Some people are more allergic to urushiol than others.

The poison ivy rash is red. It is raised and has blisters. Sometimes the skin around the rash will swell. After a few days, the blisters may break open. They might ooze a little, and then they crust over like a scab. Your rash should go away in about two weeks.

Even if you don't like the way the rash looks,
it is better to leave it uncovered. ▶

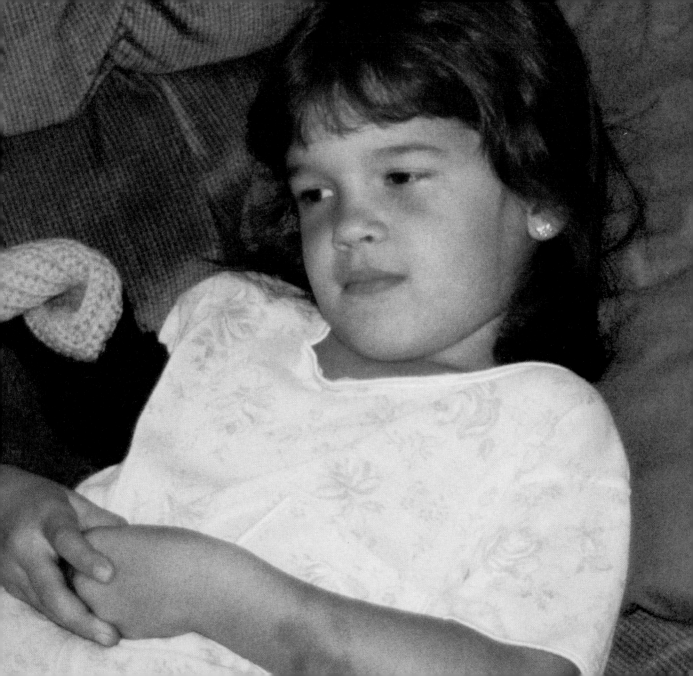

First Aid for Poison Ivy

If you touch poison ivy, don't touch anything else until you wash your hands and any other area of your body that might have touched the poison ivy.

Once you get the rash, try not to scratch it. To stop the itching, you can put a special lotion called **calamine** lotion on the rash. You can also take medicine called an **antihistamine**. Sometimes putting a cool washcloth on the rash will make it feel better.

Dabbing calamine lotion on your rash feels cool and soothing.

Washing Up

Urushiol stays **potent** for a very long time. Unless it is washed off, it can cause a rash up to five years after something has touched it. Anything that touches poison ivy, like garden tools, your clothes and shoes, or your dog, will have urushiol on it until you wash it off. If you think you've touched poison ivy, wash yourself and your things, including your clothes, right away.

If you think you've gotten urushiol on your skin, it's best to scrub with very warm water and a strong soap. ▶

Poison Oak

Poison Sumac

Partners in Crime

There are other plants that cause the same problems as poison ivy. Two of the most common ones are called poison oak and **poison sumac**. These plants contain urushiol, just as poison ivy does.

Poison oak grows as a shrub, small tree, or vine. Its leaves grow in clumps of three. Poison sumac is a tall shrub with seven to thirteen long, pointed leaves on each branch. When you're in the woods, look out for these plants the way you look out for poison ivy.

◀ *Poison oak is most commonly found in the western United States. Poison sumac is most common in the Southeast.*

Poison Ivy Facts

These are some things you might like to know about poison ivy and urushiol.

- Urushiol is colorless or light yellow.
- It takes only a tiny bit of urushiol to start an itchy rash.
- Poison ivy usually grows east of the Rocky Mountains in the United States.
- Poison ivy grows on vines or in shrubs.

Urushiol is in the stem, leaves, and roots of the poison ivy plant. ▶

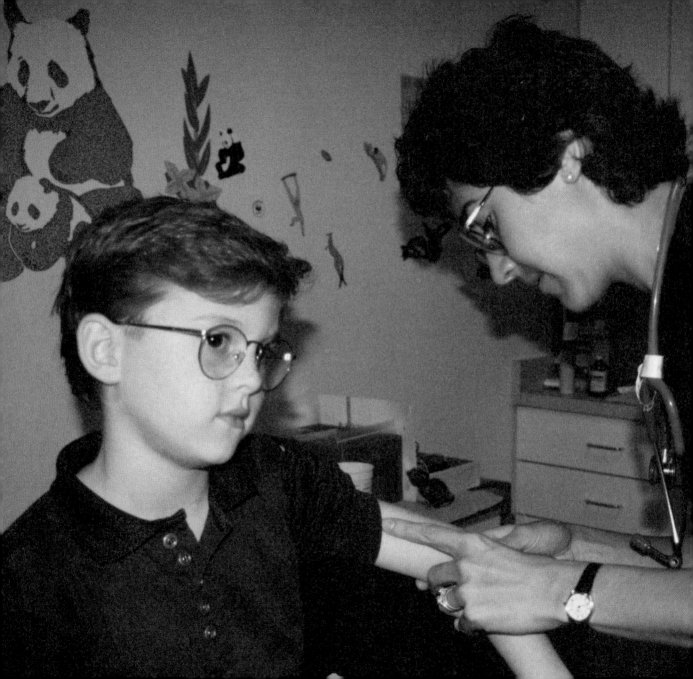

Call the Doctor!

Usually you can take care of a poison ivy rash at home. But sometimes you may need your doctor. Call the doctor if your rash is on a large part of your body, is very bad, or is on your face or near your eyes. You should also call the doctor if you've had a bad reaction to poison ivy before. Your doctor may give you medicine to help your rash go away.

◀ *You should also visit the doctor if your rash hurts or is making you very uncomfortable.*

Be Smart About Poison Ivy

Don't feel bad if you get poison ivy. It happens to lots of people. But you can try to **avoid** getting a rash. Wear long sleeves and pants if you think you'll be near poison ivy. If you're not sure if a plant is poison ivy, don't touch it. If you think you've touched poison ivy, wash your hands right away. And never put wild plants, leaves, or berries in your mouth. Following these rules will help you stay itch-free when you play in the woods!

Glossary

allergic (uh-LER-jik) Having a bad reaction to something.

antihistamine (ant-ee-HIS-tuh-meen) Medicine used to stop itching, runny noses, and watery eyes.

avoid (uh-VOYD) To stay away from something.

calamine (KA-luh-myn) A kind of lotion that soothes an itchy rash.

characteristic (kar-ik-tuh-RIS-tik) A special quality that makes something different from others like it.

poison ivy (POY-zun EYE-vee) A plant that has three leaves and causes a rash when touched.

poison sumac (POY-zun SOO-mak) A plant that causes a red, itchy rash when touched.

potent (POH-tint) Strong.

urushiol (yoo-ROO-shee-awl) The oil in poison ivy, poison oak, and poison sumac that causes an itchy rash.

Index